# small talk

# small talk

wisdom from the mouths of babes

edited by anne howard

Published in the United States in 2005
by Tangent Publications
an imprint of
Axis Publishing Limited
8c Accommodation Road
London NW11 8ED
www.axispublishing.co.uk

Creative Director: Siân Keogh
Editorial Director: Anne Yelland
Production Manager: Jo Ryan

ISBN 1-904707-28-9

2 4 6 8 10 9 7 5 3 1

Printed and bound in China

# about this book

*Small Talk* brings together a humorous selection of phrases uttered by children and their parents and complements them with gently amusing photographs.

Children love words, but sometimes try them out for size before they have fully grasped their meaning. They mishear adults, and misunderstand situations, often with amusing results. But they also have their own unique take on life, their families and friends, and concepts such as love and marriage.

This book will make you smile and help to restore a little of a child's sense of wonder to an ordinary day.

# about the author

Anne Howard is an experienced author and editor with several years publishing experience, who specializes in books on pregnancy and childcare. From the many hundreds of contributions that were sent to her, including some from her own daughter, she has selected the ones that best sum up what a child's life is all about—the joys, the quirks, and the new take on the world a small child offers.

The sun knows when I get up so it gets up every morning just before me.

I don't want to wear socks today.
I just want to wear my feet.

It's OK to drink the water in our house because flirtation makes it safe.

I like it when we go to the fish and chip shop. I love fish…

…I just don't like the white stuff inside.

Don't ever be too
full for dessert.

I had to go to the hospital to get the fraction in my wrist fixed.

It's so hot in some places that people there have to live someplace else.

Mom tells me to
behave all the time.
I hate it because
I am being-have.

Never tell your little brother that you're not going to do what your Mom told you to do.

The last letter is Z
but what is the last number?

Why didn't the three bears call the police when they found someone in their house?

Today I learned how to
make babies…

…you just change
the -y to -ies.

My teacher told me mushrooms grow in damp places.

Is that why they look like umbrellas?

My teacher got married during vacation; her husband's called the broom.

I learned in geography last week that paper is made from trees, so I guess the lines on the paper tell me how old the tree was.

Our teacher told us all about a thing she called the rain cycle and then asked us to draw a picture. She liked my picture of me on my bike in the rain so much that it made her laugh.

Unhappiness is so
unhappy that you feel
like a cat that is lost.

When you're happy
you look nice,
but when you're sad
you look horrible.

Twenty-three is the best age to get married because you know the person forever by then.

If you want someone to really love you, yell out that you love them at the top of your voice and don't worry if their parents hear you.

When you love someone,
your eyelashes go up and down
quickly and little stars
come out of you.

When someone loves you,
they say your name differently.
You know your name is safe
in their mouth.

Happiness is like a disease that grows on you. Some people more than others.

Mom, can we go to Megan's house?

I need to know where she lives before I marry her.

If you want someone
to fall in love with you,
tell them you own lots
of candy stores.

If falling in love is like learning how to spell, I don't want to do it. It takes too long.

When you fall in love I think you're supposed to get shot with an arrow or something…

…I hope it's not too sore.

Love is when you tell a guy
you like his shirt,
then he wears it every day.

Love is when Mommy
gives Daddy the best
piece of chicken.

I don't know why Daddy wears his fancy black and white suit when he goes out.

It nearly always gives him a headache the next day.

I was shopping with my Dad and
saw a sign called menswear.
I don't see what men swearing
has to do with shopping or even
why they swear in the first place.

Watching football must be really boring because my dad always goes to sleep.

Why can't dad just tell the bill people he has to play with his little boy so they'll have to wait a while for him to work?

Look dad, here's a picture
of you holding a baby of me.

Have I got it right that
Dad is Mom's husband and
Mom is Dad's life?

My Mom told me last night she loves me to pieces, so I told her I love her to crumbs.

Mommy tells me that the secret to closing my coat is to get the left part of the zipper to fit in the other side before I try to pull it up…

…I don't know why it has to be a secret.

Mom sometimes tells me that
I put my shoes on the wrong feet
but they are the only feet I have.

I saw one of Mommy's magazines yesterday and asked her what it was for. She said it tells girls how to make themselves look pretty. This is silly because it's obvious all they have to do is smile.

I know all about adoption because I was adopted…

…It means I grew in my Mommy's heart, not her tummy.

Mommy, which one
is my sweet tooth?

My Mom told me if I ever needed help I should ask a policeman so today I asked the policeman to tie my shoelace.

Mommy was telling me how she used to skate on the ice pond, play on a swing made from a tire, ride on ponies, and pick wild raspberries.
I wish I'd known her sooner.

Grandma, when I grow up I want to be as pretty as you used to be.

A grandmother is a lady who has no children of her own so likes looking after other people's.

A grandfather is a man grandmother.

My grandma told me that she
can't remember what age
she will be this year…


…I told her to look in her
underwear. Mine says I'm four.

My Mom's not having
a girl or a boy.

She's having a baby.

I don't have any brothers
or sisters…

…I'm the lonely child.

I was promised a new brother
to play with but all he
does is sleep and cry.

Anyone who says they sleep like a baby has never had a baby.

Any parent knows the easiest way to get kids to eat greens is to claim they are bad for you.

Children are naturally sticky,
even when just bathed.

Parents were created for their kids to ignore.

Why does a child on a merry-go-round wave at his parents every time he passes them…

…and why do they always wave back?

The quickest way to
get a child's attention
is to look comfortable.

Children naturally mimic their parents, no matter how hard you try to teach them good manners.

Children teach you a lot:
how much patience you
have, for example.

The only time my kid will happily do any chores is bedtime.

Children wear out parents even faster than they wear out shoes.

Thank you for my baby brother
God, but I really wanted a puppy.